# Maya's Race Against Doubt

### by Kugu Scott

**First Edition**

ISBN 979-8-89297-044-0

95 Percent Group LLC

475 Half Day Road, Suite 350 ▪ Lincolnshire, IL 60069

847-499-8200

95percentgroup.com

Printed in the United States of America.

10 9 8 7 6 5 4 3 2 1

R1.8.24

# Table of Contents

## Chapter 1

# Race Against Time

# Race Against Time

## Closed Single-Syllable Words and Consonant Blends & Digraphs

### Closed syllable words
**(including digraphs)**

bed
clock
had
win
get
ten
rush
toss
shot

### Consonant blends

| | |
|---|---|
| jumped | just |
| must | scanned |
| slept | last |
| skilled | spot |
| best | hands |
| drive | crack |
| plan | |
| cramming | |
| dragged | |

| | |
|---|---|
| smashed | snack |
| track | brush |
| black | crash |
| struck | smacked |

### High-frequency words

| Regular | Irregular | |
|---|---|---|
| opened | have | thought |
| out | already | walked |
| going | from | minutes |
| ready | whoever | said |
| herself | would | wanted |
| forward | one | again |
| around | hour | could |

### Challenge words

| | |
|---|---|
| eyes | remember |
| alarm | forgot |
| snooze | early |
| important | area |
| student | racers |
| athletes | foot |
| nearby | floor |
| runner | pushed |

Beep, beep!

Maya opened her eyes
and jumped out of bed.

The sun was already up!
She glanced at her alarm
clock. She must have smashed
the snooze and slept in!

Maya had a very important track meet that day. She was going to race skilled student athletes from nearby schools.

Whoever was the best runner would be placed on the best track team. Maya had to win.

The track meet started at 11 AM, so she had one hour to get ready and drive to the meet.

That's not bad. I can get dressed in an hour, Maya thought.

But then, her mother walked in. "Maya, remember our plan. We need to leave in ten minutes," she said.

Maya forgot the plan!
Maya and her mom wanted
to get to the track early.

Maya started to rush
again, cramming on anything
she could find.

Ten minutes later, Maya tossed her black shoes into the car, then dragged herself in.

Once Maya had a second to think in the car, it struck her that she needed a snack.

Even worse, her hair brush! How was she going to go out in front of the crowd like this?

Maya's mother pulled into the track field and told her, "Just go out there and do your best!"

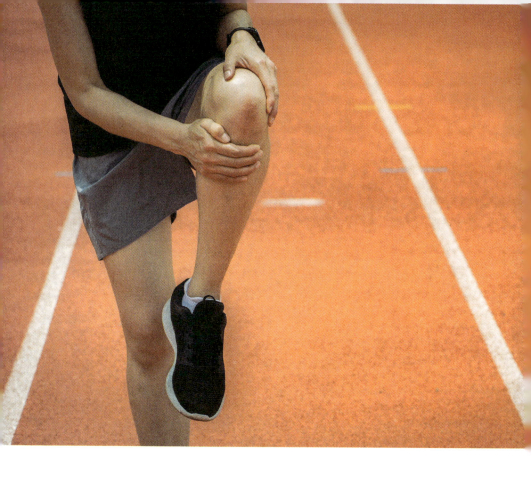

They made it just in time. She scanned the area and saw that all the other racers were waiting on the field.

Maya got in the last spot
and wiped her clammy hands.

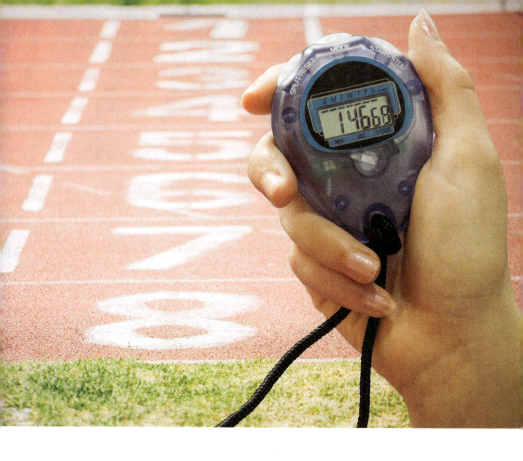

Crack! Maya's foot shot off the floor and her hands pushed her forward. She looked around.

Everyone was behind her. She was winning. She was really winning!

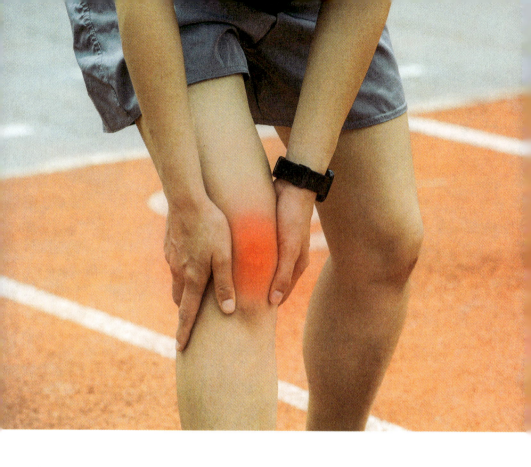

Crash! She smacked the floor.

# Chapter 2

# Maya's Unwanted Friend

# Maya's Unwanted Friend

## Long Vowel Sounds

### Silent-e

| | |
|---|---|
| waste | otherwise |
| race | stone |
| shame | pride |
| face | close |
| place | blame |
| athlete | shine |

### Open syllables

a
so
she
try

### High-frequency words

#### Regular

later
nothing

#### Irregular

| | |
|---|---|
| because | only |
| didn't | around |
| friends | |
| again | |
| good | |
| otherwise | |
| come | |

### Challenge words

| | |
|---|---|
| believe | guess |
| shoelaces | though |
| school's | student |
| Monday | writing |
| weekend | prepared |
| ruined | doubt |
| shoe | gone |
| library | shadow |

"Wow, I can't believe the school's fastest runner lost a race because of untied shoelaces."

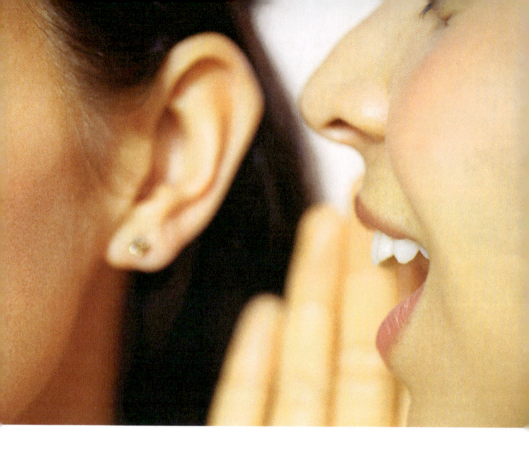

"What a shame. I'm so sad for her."

Maya walked into school on Monday with her head down. She didn't have the strength to face her friends.

That weekend, Maya's chances at the track team were ruined, all because of her untied shoe.

Maya tried to explain herself to the track coach after the race. He just told her she could try to place again next year.

Later that day after
school, Maya was sitting with
her friends in the library.

"I guess I'm not that good
of an athlete after all," she
told them.

Even though they tried to convince her otherwise, Maya's thoughts were set in stone.

She was just a bad
athlete. Maybe she was a bad
student, too.

Was she a bad friend?
What else was she bad at?

Was her writing good enough to turn in? Did she really think she was prepared for her math test?

Maya's pride was so hurt
that she began to shut down.
She felt a storm of
self-doubt come close.

She felt like nothing she did was as good, and she only had herself to blame.

Her shine was gone. Now, there was a sad shadow all around her.

# Chapter 3

# Shadow of Doubt

# Shadow of Doubt

## Vowel Teams

## Vowel teams

| | | | |
|---|---|---|---|
| dreary | fail | way | fear |
| few | day | fail | weight |
| saw | cheer | feeling | clear |
| great | eating | weak | cool |
| see | food | feet | knew |
| goals | mood | reached | weeks |
| brief | feel | afraid | peace |

## High-frequency words

### Regular

family
after

### Irregular

| | |
|---|---|
| always | does |
| around | have |
| everything | everyone |
| friends | once |
| only | |
| would | |
| out | |
| again | |

## Challenge words

| | |
|---|---|
| following | tomorrow |
| mornings | thoughts |
| positive | carry |
| excited | confidence |
| moment | |
| science | |
| shoelaces | |
| practice | |
| door | |

A few more times, Maya saw a dreary shadow always following her around.

In the mornings, Maya tried to focus on positive things. Everything was great. She was excited to see her friends.

She had goals in life. But
her mind was happy for only
a brief moment. Then it raced
back to that big fail.

Science was Maya's best subject. Even if she was having a bad day, science would cheer her up.

But this time, even science would not take the track fail out of her mind.

It felt set in her mind.

"But why?" Maya asked.
Her untied shoelaces had
nothing to do with science.

Later, when she was
eating food with her family,
Maya got in a sad mood
again.

I don't know why I feel this way, she thought. What does food have to do with my fail?

Maya tried to go on practice runs, but she had too much on her mind.

Feeling weak, she kept on checking her shoelaces and looking at her feet.

By the time she reached for the door, Maya decided to run again tomorrow. She was afraid.

Maya became scared by
her worries, thoughts, and
fear of messing up.

When she walked into a room, her dark shadow came first.

The weight was too much
for her to carry.

It was clear that this Maya was not the cool girl everyone once knew.

A few weeks after the race, Maya felt a peace and confidence that she had not felt in a long time.

That morning, she went
for a run at the park.

# Chapter 4

# A Magical Bond

# A Magical Bond

## Consonant-le + Vowel-r

### Consonant-le

mumbled
puzzle
jumble

### Vowel-r

| | |
|---|---|
| hard | hurt |
| arms | short |
| her | girl |
| dart | park |
| far | scarred |
| start | share |
| scared | |

### High-frequency words

| Regular | Irregular |
|---|---|
| toward | thought |
| about | one |
| | other |
| | used |
| | could |
| | anything |
| | said |
| | were |

### Challenge words

| | |
|---|---|
| foot | fault |
| practice | sorry |
| ahead | reaction |
| important | schools |
| shoelaces | silent |
| floor | accident |
| happening | doubt |
| Isabelle | confidence |
| control | emotions |

How hard can this be?
Maya thought. One foot, then
the other.

Without practice, Maya's arms did not help her dart far ahead like they used to.

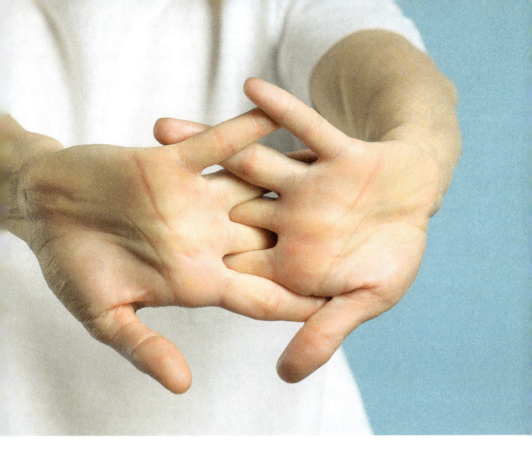

But it was important for
her to start.

Too scared to look up while running, Maya looked down at her shoelaces.

Crash! Maya smacked the floor.

*This can't be happening again!* Maya thought.

But before she could
say anything, a blurry hand
reached toward her.

"Are you okay? Are you hurt?" A short girl with long hair was looking at Maya like she was a puzzle.

"We bumped into each other. I'm Isabelle."

"I think it was my fault. Sorry. I'm not a good runner," mumbled Maya.

In fact, it was Isabelle who bumped into Maya. Isabelle took note of Maya's reaction.

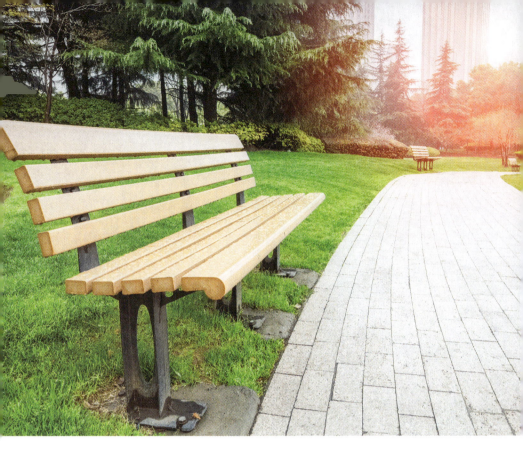

Both of them went to sit on the park bench.

They asked each other
which schools they went
to, and about their favorite
subjects.

When Isabelle asked about
the sports Maya liked, Maya
fell silent.

"What went wrong?" asked Isabelle.

"It's nothing. I just had an epic fail a few weeks ago at a big race."

"Now I'm sad and scarred," said Maya. "Nothing has been the same since."

"I know how you feel,"
said Isabelle. "I had a race
accident a few years ago."

"I let my self-doubt jumble my confidence, and I hit rock bottom. I had to learn to trust myself and control my emotions again."

Maya listened. For the first time, Maya felt like someone got her.

"I learned something with my shadow of doubt. If you want, I can share about it," said Isabelle.

From that point on,
Isabelle and Maya were a
pair.

**Kugu Scott** enjoys writing about critical global issues, supporting children's rights, volunteering, and taking part in civil services projects. Her two Storyshares books received honorable mention awards in the 2021 and 2022 Storyshares Story of the Year Contests. She is a Congressional Award Gold Medal and STEM STAR recipient. She is the winner of the 2022 European Union Year of the Youth Writing Contest, judged by the European Parliament members, and has taken part in volunteering projects such as Ukrainian War Refugees Camp in Belgium, EU Youth Development Program in Germany, European Communities Ethnic, Cultural, and Religious program in Israel. She is a member of the European Union Youth Forum and UNICEF USA Advocate, where she acts as the voice for young people and strives for societies where young people are empowered and encouraged to achieve their fullest potential as global citizens.

Storyshares is focused on supporting older striving readers by creating a new shelf in the library specifically for them. The ever-growing collection features content that is compelling and culturally relevant for older students, teens, and adults, yet still readable at a range of lower reading levels.

Storyshares generates content by engaging deeply with writers, bringing together a community to create this new kind of book. With more intriguing and approachable stories to choose from, striving readers are improving their skills and beginning to discover the joy of reading. For more information, visit storyshares.org.

Easy to Read. Hard to Put Down.